American Fractal

American Fractal

Poetry

Timothy Green

RED HEN PRESS | Los Angeles, California

American Fractal

Book layout by Jeff Takaki

ISBN: 978-1-59709-130-5

Library of Congress Catalog Card Number: 2008929839

The City of Los Angeles Cultural Affairs Department, Los Angeles
County Arts Commission, California Arts Council and the National
Endowment for the Arts partially support Red Hen Press.

Published by Red Hen Press

www.redhen.org

First Edition

Printed in Canada

ACKNOWLEDGEMENTS

The author is grateful to the journals where these poems, sometimes in earlier versions, first appeared:

Blood Orange Review: "High on Hog"; *Caduceus:* "Apocrypha" and "A Tourist's Guide Through Big Sky Country"; *Confrontation:* "Hiking Alone" and "Hiking Together"; *Connecticut Review:* "Poem from Dark Matter," "Fifty-Hour Online Gaming Binge Proves Fatal" and "Playing Our Part"; *Crab Creek Review:* "The Memory of Water"; *Cranky:* "Poem for the Valentines," "The Sense of Being Looked At" and "Pot Luck"; *Cutthroat:* "Poem from the Homeland"; *Diner:* "Some Proof" and "Thanksgiving Was Over"; *Euphony:* "On the Phone My Mother"; *Florida Review:* "The Space of One Nap"; *Fugue:* "Her Face Once"; *Gargoyle:* "Diorama"; *H_ngm_n:* "The Urge to Break Things"; *HazMat Review:* "A Constant Lack of Hunger"; *Hiram Poetry Review:* "The Good Times"; *Los Angeles Review:* "Applauding the Gods"; *Lungful!:* "Cheers"; *Mid-American Review:* "The Body" and "Pluots and Apriums"; *Nimrod International Journal:* "Impressionism" and "The Bending of Birches"; *Paterson Literary Review:* "Man Auctions Ad-Space on Forehead"; *Pearl:* "Saddled"; *Pedestal Magazine:* "After Hopper"; *Poetry Midwest:* "Microcassette" and "White Noise"; *Rattle:* "Cooking Dinner"; *Rock Salt Plum Review:* "Midnight Mass" and "To Montevideo"; *Runes:* "American Fractal"; *Subtropics:* "What Passes for Optimism at MacArthur Park"; *Slipstream:* "Beach Scene"; *Spillway:* "Beating Balaam's Ass" and "2.9."

With deep appreciation and gratitude to my teachers, editors, and friends in poetry: Alan Fox, Erik Campbell, Jim Ragan, James Longenbach, Barbara Jordan, Kate Gale, and, above all others and always, Megan O'Reilly.

for Megan

CONTENTS

V

I

It turns out that an eerie type of chaos can lurk just behind a façade of order—and yet, deep inside the chaos lurks an even eerier type of order.
—Douglas Hofstadter

THE BODY

in the dream I wake to a poem about trains   what it is that insists

that crawls   clamors   the windowpane clasped shut against a

wind   outside bare branches in a dry heave & I rise   over the

swelling resolution   not to rise   I rise   consider the light

switch   consider the electric blanket warmth   I rise instead

go to the window which is no longer a window but a box full of

moonlight   & down there in the meadow   just a handful of

starspecks in the foxglove   her hair is blue grass   & the first thing

I think of are the wet walls of howe caverns   that tourist trap back

east   the pipe organ   the bridal altar   the river styx

stalactites & stalagmites fusing   the slow settle of limestone

bicarbonate   a blind bat on a billboard unfurling leather wings

unfurling night   unleashing a gust of   supersonic transience

an old dog's call to supper   *twenty miles to go*   *fifteen*   *get*

your wallet ready   & there it is again   the unmistakable whistle the bleating   the bleeding   the letting off of steam   & she's by

the tracks with something in her hands   a silver shining thing &

through the silent distance   through the square hole in my bedroom

wall   I know there's nothing left to call it but hope   though it's

just a quarter   a nickel   a dime   general washington's hope

your twenty-five cents worth of hope   a handful of gum balls   a

plastic egg full of costume jewelry that would stain a tiny finger green

it's just the sedimentary   the sentimental dream token hope   the

hope you go to hell   the hope you forgive me   the hope you

remember to hope at least   love   & she sets it down on the far

track as if dropping her hope into the cool slot of a jukebox   the low

clink clambers up from inside my throat   as she steps over   both

tracks   over the shimmering shining thing   over the glittering

fluttering tumbling turning thing now lifting at its edges   the thing

that's always more than whatever it is because   there's the whistle again   the rumble   a distant thunder   because the past can't

hold the future   the present rumbles on   *five miles almost there*

hush now   it sweeps past   two geometric lines that never touch

& there's the lamplight   the steamstack   the hot metal glow

& at her heels this unnameable sadness   this burden   the eternal

space there between the train's first passing   & the wind that follows

a second later   to wake the body   from its only available dream

THANKSGIVING WAS OVER

so she baked Christmas cookies while he trapped
    the last bee in a jar. At the kitchen window

it barely buzzed, half-hibernating, his hand unstung
    forever always, he assured, the bee

dreaming itself somewhere else—the heart
    of a hive, perhaps, at the height of summer's heat.

And so he let it go like a wish in the woods.
    And so she let it go like a drop of honey.

Milk poured slow-motion in a glass behind them,
    too thick to be real. And the gingerbread men

wore their charred feet, doughy scars;
    they smiled through mouths of molasses.

And so they ate each other there, crumb by crumb,
    until they weighed too much to carry.

SOME PROOF

Large as goose feathers, carbon-copy flowers cut themselves
from the lawn with invisible scissors, crinkle up intricate

origami at our feet. Some men ready the wheelbarrow,
put out all their pots and hats. Others take to fire—that older

God—make coal out of ash to warm their toes. In the garden
we gather notes—inkstains, papercuts—give meaning

to the flood like Noah. No one needs papyrus to write it down
and all language is pictographic. Sometimes it rains receipts

in duplicate, triplicate. Each pink slip like a teardrop is fully
tax deductible. Sometimes the shorter stubs pass between us

lovingly, with little embarrassment, like gifts.

To Montevideo

for L.

We were double-sided tape, she writes,
all adhesive. We were the hollow space

a shell curls around; the wrapping
that is the gift. Like children boiling tea

from pine needles, it wasn't a thirst
that moved us. You chased a soccer ball

around the world while I chased the world.
We were like your speech—blunt and broken,

only as beautiful as it was meaningless.
No way to say it more simply than that.

As her new husband stirs upstairs
she folds the letter. Tongues the glue.

"Fifty-Hour Online Gaming Binge Proves Fatal"

in memory of Lee Seong Seop

Think of Miller: "When you forget to eat
you know that you're alive." Think of Einstein's
ant farm, eight hours, his thick nose on the glass.
Mileva called from the kitchen, from the street,
Novi Sad—it didn't matter. Some kinds
of men just live inside their heads, like bass
thrown back twice, like flies in love with fly sheets.
Like Lee, my father drowns in penny wine.
Like Lee, my brother smokes his mellow grass.
Like Lee, we choke down every little sweet
we find, our eyes on any stone that shines
as if this bit of light could never last.
And even when it doesn't, all is well:
One finds a pearl, another just the shell.

HIP

His nickname not for how cool he was
in the sixties, nor his sense of style.
Not for a love of architecture's angles,
long summers leaning on roof peaks,
a dozen nails between his teeth. No,
my father was Hip only because he
broke his
        surfing, he said, through
the hurricane of a youth in Florida
where the water split blue to green and
all nurse sharks and pool sharks looked
the same. He had a way of telling stories
slumped in his recliner like a late-night
talk show host mid-monologue, every
punch line the pearl around some tiny
truth.
        Everyone knew the real story:
hit by a car walking to school, a whole
year in plaster only his sister would sign.
Not a friend to rename him, no one
to note the irony, pat him playfully
on the back. My grandmother fed him
pudding, held the glass while he sucked
milk through a straw.
            He must have
spent that time dreaming up other lives—
I don't blame him. Four walls around
a solitude and with the curtains drawn

it isn't real. And so I draw my curtains.
So, too, I shut the light and leave—
not fitting in any room like my father
never fit, shoulders stiff, a janitor's
loop of keys already digging at my hip.

MIDNIGHT MASS

He maketh me lie down in green pastures:
He leadeth me beside still waters.
—Psalm 23

Misplaced mutt. No collar. Napping. Fur like
       mother's mitten
    in my hand, tugging her

only child home. Church bells in the moon-
       light, false witness,
    snow. I remember asking

Were there any dogs in Bethlehem? The Lord
       then my shepherd,
    confused at five. That life

lying among statues so quiet, so calm in its
       Christmas coat.
    Breath like a hymn. Wet nose,

nostrils flaring slow. How could any-
       thing so fragile
    live on its own, no nest, no

soul inside it? Like a babe in the woods I
       wanted to bring it
    back with us. Yet we kept

walking. Past the chapel, past the churchyard
      the lumberyard,
        the train tracks and their

bed of stone. I can't remember what she said.
      Fear of fleas, perhaps
        it may be feral; whatever it was

made sense I'm sure. We didn't need another
      dog, didn't have
        room in our little house for

another mouth to feed. *But were they there*
      in Bethlehem, I
        insisted, *Would Mary tell Jesus*

No? I was a brat. A spoiled prince, enthroned.
      But when I close
        my eyes I see that mutt in

the manger. Starving, lonely and cold. Wisemen
      around him stuffed
        with straw, unmoving. My

mother making sense. One footprint falling
      into the next.

Her Face Once

imagine dusk   a streetcar   your empty

window   sheets of rain coating glass   your

hand   riddled with age   peels back the

thick skin of an orange   as in the city below

your past is slipping past unnoticed in the scores

of headlights   you move to shut the blinds

but don't   there was truth once you tell

yourself   there was the mold & then ash

settling in the kiln   you saw her face once in

marble   in granite   her face chiseled on

the face of some mountain   somewhere

you'd never been   in a clay bowl you poured

by hand   in a catch-try for the orange peels

for the collection of acid & rind   & you try to

piece things back together   one by one   try

to stop time & speak backward in tongues   to

bind the vinyl coat with wax   you close your

eyes & imagine decay dissolving   fruit

falling up to the branch & striking with enough

force to fuse stem & wood   but things don't

move that way   here   gravity pulling from

the center   three dimensions collapsing in

two like a photograph   as your only love

slips by unnoticed among the passing headlights

her face glinting with rain like polished stone

a stranger   on a streetcar   at dusk

It can be demonstrated with thermo-
    luminescence: the salt solution
retains knowledge of what it once held,
    though nature, though logic
would tell it otherwise. Dumb as a bedpan,
    the hydrogen bond remembers
the lithium, the sodium chloride no matter
    how long distilled. There is so
little purity left in the world. Desire it,
    dilute it, strip it down till nothing
remains, onion eyes wept dry, last flake
    of the artichoke bit clean,
sour stalk swallowed whole. The homeopath
    stirs his mug, glass rod
guiding poison to balm, balm to poison,
    nothing settling, nothing
dispelled. With every loss the ache
    of a phantom limb he never
believed in. Still he finds himself
    awake at night, clutching the
cool insistence of a pillow to his chest.

POEM FROM THE HOMELAND

Rose Bowl, 2006

As she trills
the last note,
there's smoke.

Each song now
taken literally.

When the fire-
crackers burst,
we leap to our

relief. We clap,
put our fingers

in our teeth. Then
the B-1 Lancer
in the twilight.

Drum-roll of
the turbofans,

their heat.

II

So, nat'ralist observe,
A flea hath smaller fleas that on him prey,
And these have smaller fleas to bite 'em,
And so proceed ad infinitum.
—Jonathan Swift

Poem from Dark Matter

First light through the limbs of the trees. And then
the trees. Each morning the hum of traffic
through the freeway wall. And then the traffic

we're bottled in. Each thing first betrayed
by the shapes around it. As if shadows held
all our weight. Like the empty space that props

each fiery nest of stars, the smooth circumference
of every heavenly body toward which astronomers
might dream. I'm at the kitchen window, early light.

Reading science for tea leaves. Pluto, it seems,
is far colder than we thought. Even the constant
speed of light is decaying. And look where thoughts

can lead: Somewhere in a lonely future, a man
hears his heart stop beating long before the world
goes black. So slow the rate at which nothing

approaches. Or maybe like an ostrich we'll outrun
our past. And then our present. And this, my gift
to you, whatever you'll make of it: The soul, a ship

in a bottle lost at sea. Drops its anchor anyway.

Poem for the Valentines

Iridescent in the intersection
of Laurel and Burbank,

a lime vest bobs like a charm
without a chain. Two hands

holding flares guide the idle
traffic home, while overhead

in the apple-picker an electrician
works his quiet length of cord.

In lieu of flowers, he thinks,
the redundancy of the grid:

Just this one signal gone limp
in the wind. While far outside

the darkness, a delicate nose licks
at the petals of a rose; a pair of

lobsters are waiting for the pot.

Hiking Alone

I shimmy out on sandstone and slate rock,
past the soft ledges where the last shrubs

grow. I've got my camera, unshuttered and
silent, ready to take back with me whatever

I've come here for—sore arms and a sunburn,
blue sky like something new. At the floor

of the canyon far below a stream flows from
nowhere to nothing, from one unseen cavern

to the next. I could think of a fish gazing up
at that quick flash of sky as it passes through

the white froth of the rapids, the silky silver
where the water pools. *Oh, I am grey*, I could

have him say, personified—moved, even
full of emotion. *Oh, my scales are golden-*

green—I could give him color just as easily
in the kind God of my imagination before

plunging him back into his comfortable
dark, this eyelet the only opening for miles.

How easy it is to paint epiphany, I think, like
the gaudy sunset now settling above the tree-

line I could call a bruise or a blush, windburn
on a woman's cheek, though it's only the

scattering of dust in low light, what one shakes
from a shoe, combs out of stiffened hair.

How easy, too, it would be to slip off this ledge,
to get lost out here, fall asleep on this rock and

let the cold night wake me. I could hold out
on figs and freshwater; I could chew the fibrous

bark off a Joshua tree. I could love the moon
like a mountain lion, stalk shadows, sharpen

sticks. Come morning I'd find the dirt road
and then my car at the end of it. Brush the dust

off my pants. Buckle myself back into habit
with a metal click like the sound of my one hand

clapping for joy—however briefly—at all we
ever wanted: a little darkness to climb out of.

HIKING TOGETHER

It isn't the exertion or the triumph.
It isn't the heavy breath set down
on stone, shared rhythm of our
walking, the curve of your ass I
follow. It isn't the sudden clearing
and the butterflies, bronze light at
the summit—though still I wonder
what makes these gold bugs beautiful,
what other insect would I hold
past my senseless fear of insects?
One clings to my shoulder now,
paper wings like a folded note.
It isn't fragility, the briefness of
a bloom, perfection of the day,
or how long we watch them play
in the light, soft bodies pressing
over and over like pairs of hands.
It isn't your tongue in my mouth.
Nor even this photograph, still at
the base, your fear of heights hidden
behind a blue hoodie, hip cocked—
already queen of the mountain.

Beach Scene

Phillip C. Curtis, 1962

Everywhere their clothes are coming apart, falling
          off. The wind
     blows silk shreds of confetti.

At the beach, a gray gull circles, eyeing the glitter,
          the glitz, the pink
     tassels like intestines fishermen

leave in heaps at the pier. One thing is always
          mistaken for
     another, as if accident were

the fundamental attribute of life—lightning strikes
          a rock, the rock
     becomes a heart, the heart

fits perfectly inside the hollow tomb of your chest
          as you watch
     their clothes come off, stitch by

painful stitch. That thumping, sputtering organ
          kicks and purrs
     one more time like it's New Year's

Eve in New Jersey, and everyone left in the room
          stops at once
     to moisten their perfectly parted lips.

2.9

Four months on a faultline
and then you see it coming.

The far floor, a brick wall, rising
up to greet you, pulling back.

A slow tide, a second thought.

A gesture you've seen before
but can never place: the scent

of a lemon tree, of low light.

And as you wonder—*Where?*
Where?—that little tremor

touches your sleeve, lets go.

What Passes for Optimism at MacArthur Park

Beside the concrete pond, small children fish
for nothing. This is all it costs to wish:
a yard of yarn, a crooked stick. They cast
their paper cups as if they might outlast
hunger, as if a minnow might appear
from muck and shoes and empty cans of beer.
We watch them scoop up all the trash that floats.
We watch the lovers on their paddle boats
like swans, like swans! the little children holler.
We have our picture taken for a dollar.
While on the gravel path the pigeons scatter
for crumbs, their tiny feet a kind of chatter
so empty and so full of soft demands
that everyone, not listening, understands.

How I'd Explain It

Love like a mercy kill,
like the bait and shoot of deer

that would starve themselves
otherwise. This is for

your own good, he thinks,
his finger numb

as it pulls the trigger.
The doe never bends toward

the apple core
whose scent drew her; she waits

in the warm clearing as if
she knows

what's coming.
And sometimes

I think maybe she does.

Playing Our Part

Under peaceful conditions a
warlike man sets upon himself.
—Friedrich Nietzsche

He hasn't left his hut on the hill in so long
no one remembers his face. Some say at night

he unfurls his beard like a tattered scroll
and reads himself to sleep. Others claim age

has outlasted gender, that nothing human stirs
between his legs—male and female, alpha and

omega, he is everything at once. What is certain
is that there is no certainty beyond his gaze;

he spends his days sharpening the bayonet,
measuring the time it takes to disassemble

then reassemble his assault rifle. The hands
move slow on his gold watch. Thin crosshairs

mark his chest. And so our factories whir
incessantly, mixing the sulfur, the saltpeter.

And so we bury our dead with pride.
We fight like this to keep the dream alive.

American Fractal

We are like two chasms—a well
staring up at the sky.
—Fernando Pessoa

two mirrors face each other   my hands over my face   the

porcelain soap dish   an angel's wings & a mile of its offerings

pink on pink on black tile   I'm in the bathroom   close the door

shut the light   down the hall the tv too loud   bob barker & *the*

price is right   shut that out too   I'm on the other edge of

something   of adulthood   of a gulf   a canyon   looking

down down   no vultures circling picking bones though   no

heaped bodies to climb over   no fall to cushion   or to be

cushioned   not the body that matures this time   just this

hollow wooden door   the lock my parents could pick with a belt-

hook at any moment   the hot glare of the vanity lights making

my pimples glow   *I said shut the light*   shut the light   the tv too loud mother won't get up   *get up!*   the friend visiting

from florida   her baby james sucking grapes   he wouldn't eat

anything else   just the grapes   the seedless orbs like eyeballs

sucking them   each green globe with a little pop   a little giggle

wouldn't take the formula   wouldn't take the mashed carrots &

peas   brown mush from a jar   the rubber spoon an airplane

but still nothing   a silent protest maybe   maybe reading into

things too far   we fed him grapes for three weeks   he kept

giggling   sleeping in my bedroom   a crib of blankets in the

cedar hope chest at the foot of my bed   grapes & grapes & the

husband flying up finally to take him home   to take her home

a quiet man   a mustache   all five-foot-five of him fumbling

down the hall the showcase showdown   the systolic bleep of the

wheel slowing to rest   a dinette set   a new car   flashing lights   cheers & screams from the audience   mother's best

friend in the intersection held her baby   cat-walked the dotted

yellow line & then sat down   the baby crying   the headlights

horns   she sat down   then the police call at midnight   *do you*

know the father?   then driving home holding the baby while my

father shifted & swore   the soft skull   the soft neck   way

past bedtime   past due   *stay up!*   *stay up!*   his head so

heavy   mother on the couch again won't get up   won't blink

a crack in the ceiling holding her there   mesmerized   like the

root of that word something animal   doctoral   doctor mesmer

on his glass armonica   the women in tubs of glass powder

iron filings   the magic of the wand   *relax relax*   *my sweet*

baby james   singing from behind the curtain   *go to sleep*   *go*

to sleep   they had words for it back then   *hysteria distemper*   the doctors in the waiting room more mysterious

more clinical   we had clinics now   *post-partum depression*

they said   *bipolar disorder*   they said in their white robes

behind their stethoscopes & clipboards   their shoes so soft they

moved soundlessly down the long hall *the price is right* on a

television hanging from the ceiling   I sit down in the bathtub

how can you blame them for sitting down   things getting so

heavy?   for what do we hold onto eventually?   eventually

what don't we hold onto?   mother in the living room   on the

couch   *shake her shake her*   *wake her up*   & father   at the

bar he says   late at work he says   & the bathroom with its

cheap lock   that convenient clasp   & the light on   & the

light off   & the mirror into mirror into mirror   that silver-

backed glass   looking like her   looking like him   the images playing off themselves in the glass *divide* *divide* & how

could they know each one each image into infinity how

could they know? each image one moment behind the last

catching up & catching up until the last & finally letting go

the last like a leap into no faith letting go that smallest star

that grain of sand that simplest & finest point of light

III

A hen is only an egg's way of making another egg.
—Samuel Butler

COOKING DINNER

Spring again. Its warmer breeze. Open screen door.
Another war buds up, pliant and green,
       thick spores of restlessness
like pollen in the air—you could sneeze with it;
your heart could stop beating in a moment.
    ____ bless you, you're whispering.
             ____ bless you.
As if a soul could leak like steam from its
       cellular prison, as if words alone
could draw it back—white light, white light,
a sheet, a flag.
Every day more words to be wary of, that space there
in the blessing, that monotone
on the radio with its figures and dates and facts
and facts that rattle on long after
you've pulled the plug, glued shut
       your ears, rattle on,
rat-tat-tat like something you won't say
while you drown yourself in a cold water bath,
pry loose your silver fillings
because you've heard that story—oh yes,
you've heard it before,
but maybe it's your whole body that's
transmitting their signals this time, that subsonic
       headache drone, your bones
the antennae, your marrow electric,
pulsing, mortar crumbling, bricks
knocked free, windows smashed, bits of glass

like blue gravel, tires and dumpsters
          on fire with looting, the whole world
coming loose, thin thread being
pulled and pulled, wound tight
                around your _____.
But there she is over the stove.
          Relax, she says. Just relax. She's cooking
dinner. Egg noodles and mushroom soup.
The kitchen dizzy with steam. Her apron
stained from years of fancier meals, wasted
energy, messes not worth
                    cleaning up.
Not *coming* loose, she says,
                been loose. A grocery list
of wars, holy wars, hunger.
These pots just boil with their watching, is all.
Out on the porch the clatter of a small animal,
                a neighbor's cat. The faint stir
of last year's dried-out leaves against the fence
          finally being looked at.

After Hopper

Nighthawks, 1942

She says that everything is *after* Hopper.
That posh hotel—you looked about to slap her,
but never did. Sometimes she'd wait at night
in her blue robe, face folded like the note
you didn't leave crumpled in a coat pocket.
Sometimes she'd stand in broad daylight, naked
before an open window, flesh so pale
and round and full it seemed about to pull
a tide of ruttish men up from the street.
But mostly it's the red dress. The cut straight,
sleeveless, loose. And her mouth is only lipstick.
She says you never even see her talk,
but just *about* to talk, *about* to smile.
She says that every moment is a jail;
this diner is her prison of endless light,
the ceaseless hour always getting late—
yet no one moves. Her cigarette remains
unlit. The busboy doesn't lift his hands.
You could write a thousand lines, she says,
on all the things she never does or has.
How she seems so sad she might have cried.
How you only see her *almost* satisfied.

MEDITATION ON THE SIX HEALING SOUNDS

         The refrigerator hums a perfect
middle C but offers no intent.
         The blender, the ceiling fan stir
              up trouble alternately,
flu and mold no match
         for this cold uncoiling. In the trees,
              transistors click and hiss
like vipers, an incessant
         wind in their black vines. The book
              tells me to imagine sadness
as pressure released,
         as steam from a cracked pipe.
              I visualize a mist of white
light sealing the crack,
         the shining warmth of a silver
              cloak to protect me. Healing
is a conscious process,
         the book says. Every tune needs
              attention, an orchestra
of appliances whirling into
         life, a universe of ambient noise—
              but only the mind matters,
only the self creates meaning,
         electrostatic pump firing the systole of
              joy, the diastole of anger.
Posture is everything, the book
         says. The body is a conduit
              of God, meaning all good things.
Fear is stored in the lungs.

"HIGH ON HOG"

—New York Times, Health, 8/12/05

Who knew trans-fatty acids were to blame
for our clattering hearts—like metal trays
clanging in the kitchen of the chest, fist-sized
cow bells, church bells—we nearly went insane
in bed; we tore apart our dressing gowns,
our heads between our lovers' legs to taste
the silence there. But even in that place
of little air we heard the heavy sound
of death: the pulse as such a frail machine,
what never rests. Worried, we couldn't sleep.
We counted saturated fats like sheep
and after years of choosing margarine
of course our arteries have grown too hard,
hydrogenized. So now we cook with lard.

MICROCASSETTE

At first it was just a gift, the batteries not included,
but wrapped neatly in a smaller box, a matching

bow with the same generous loop of silver, its paper
the same gaudy green. *Try it out,* she told him,

and so he did. *Is this the way I sound?* he said.
Is this the way I sound? it told him, and then

he chuckled and learned the way he chuckled.
He found that tapes were cheap and began taping

everything. On his way to work he taped the car
radio, the transmission shifting gears. At lunch

it was the cafeteria, he taped the commotion and
spent each afternoon untangling conversations

from the squeaking chairs, the clattering trays.
Sometimes he recorded his wife in bed in secret,

and he hid those tapes in the garage. But what he
loved most was his own voice, not the sound itself,

but the newness of it, the mystery of a stranger
knowing every last detail. The red light flickered

for days, which broke perfectly into 90-minute
intervals he labeled with a ballpoint pen. Soon

he realized that it wasn't one voice in there,
in his chest, but a whole colony of tones and

inflections ready to rise up and serve its purpose.
What a noble thing, he told the microphone,

this army of voices always prepared. Words
to his wife in public were different in the bedroom.

Around men there was strength in *Hello.*
Maybe he mumbled more than he'd like,

and he wasn't proud of the bar voice, but singing-in-
the-shower voice often brought a tear to his eye.

(His father voice grunted at the show of emotion.)
How easily we slough the shell of our character, he said

in the poet's voice, lifting an invisible glass of
sweet champagne—as if it were something to toast.

Pot Luck

One at a time we heap our images
onto the table: a pot luck dinner.

Someone has brought the shoplifted
wristwatch, the keyed Caddy, a dead

fish in a mailbox—Aunt Edna says
it's salmon though it looks like trout.

There are the tree limbs and toilet paper,
the dime bag of oregano, the fake ID.

I've brought a bowl of arson for
the turkey, its maniacal grin smoldering

up through cinders. From the chair
where Dad used to sit, Mom drops

a mug-shot in the mashed potatoes,
a little careless now, a tired look in her

one good eye. No one says a thing.
My brother asks me to pass the peas.

On the Phone My Mother

says she's listening, says
        have you eaten yet,
has the California sky lost its hue?

We prattle like this, we pitch, we list.

She asks and asks; I answer
everything.

A room full of hot air here;
a room full of hot air there.

And so we blow in our balloon,
happy for the hole in it.

And so the circle holds its shape,
        hovers there.

And so the silence is full
        of this thin
whistling sound.

Something escaping, always,
something holding on.

BEFORE THE FLOOD

Rain again on the radar and
    I've got the towels ready,
        tracing all the cracks.

Ruined books like bricks
    to hold them down.
        Like always it's the binding

that's first to go, glue
    seeping up the spine,
        ink turned sticky, the faces

of the text bleeding together
    like Siamese twins.
        Wet paper is twice

the weight, floating in
    dirty water like a sponge.
        But sink or swim, words

are wasted. On television
    a man from Big Bear who
        drove down to the coast

to fill his truck with sandbags.
    History relieves itself,
        he tells the reporter on-scene

and I think he means
    it shits like everyone else,
        but it could have been

Freudian. Either way
    the writing is on the wall.
        A brown line knee-deep.

DIORAMA

That summer they made chalk outlines of
      everything: on every street
the rag-doll limbs of a jumper, every bank
      with its flat pile of powder
to step over, the security guards, policemen,
      each robber with what
could have been a flower sprouting from
      the stocking on his head.

When the televisions vanished we watched
      the rectangles on our
living room floors, any ant or insect's aimless
      march the perfect metaphor
for life, until it too snuffed out like a candle
      in one brief puff of
granular nirvana, its stillness too small for
      even a calcium deposit

to wrap around. How simple then it made
      the world, one less
dimension to worry about—the walls cut down
      with the trees, all shade
symbolic. Every view was the bird's eye
      view, every path it's own
map. Imagine a straight line from wherever
      you're going to where

you used to be. Look here: This yellow patch
      was the dog my car struck.
This is the box where the car had been.

BEATING BALAAM'S ASS
Numbers 22:30

The books are wrong, you know,
and the priests—they're told only

what to tell the children. Look both
ways, don't shit where you eat, that

sort of thing. And the children listen.
And I listen. And the priests, they

listen most, their clean heads lowered
in great psalms of listening.

But heaven is a highway in Kansas.
Nothing waits: no commandments

or pearly gates; not a mighty gavel
but merely *gravel*, mile after loose

mile of it, no other soul in sight.
The geometry of the afterlife: four

corners, a stop sign. The paint on
the sign reflective, easy to read.

The thousand ears of God are ears
of corn, and none of them listen to

the only sound, which is your engine,
your one horse always approaching.

The life you're leading, being led.

IV

America is hard to see.
—Robert Frost

OLD MOTHER TARANTULA

Canyon de Chelly, Arizona

When the eggs hatch she lays a hundred more
for them to feed on—their blind eyes blood-orange,
their bodies soft and white as candle wax.
Soon they'll harden, shed shells, grow large, fast.
But now they nibble at the never-born;
they suck their siblings dry—this hungry swarm
we call a consequence of math. And when
the eggs are not enough—for what portends
to be enough, the arithmetic of flavor
so keen, the mouths so many?—the mother
spider lies among her callous kin,
offers finally herself. How then can
we not call it sacrifice? Look how still
she sits. As if embodying an ideal
were this small and simple thing. Old hat.
Who wouldn't see some magic under that?

"Man Auctions Ad Space on Forehead"

—BBC News, 1/10/05

He couldn't look at the logo until it was finished—
that was part of the publicity, camera crew on hand

recording every twitch and grimace before his money-
shot reaction to the upturned mirror. A contract

protected him from too much embarrassment: No
swastikas or racial slurs, no 666, the sign of the beast.

Most likely it would be a web address, something
catchy and trite, easy to find online. Romantics

wanted to buy him LOVE in gold block letters, like
something from a movie, a kiss at the credits, but

the bidding went high. Even his mother pooled her
assets, said she'd send him an invisible sign that read:

MORON. Secretly he hoped for the Nike Swoosh or
the Pepsi Globe, or maybe a sports-team's emblem, any

team—he'd convert. Clause 34c said he could never
again wear a hat in public: He'd have to make do.

Everyone was talking; it was the new parlor game—
what would you make him wear for the rest of his life?

A middle finger? The Yin-Yang? Would you be
generous? Would you use a scarlet font? Or maybe

would you have them print this poem. Have them print it
in a slanted scrawl, like a secret encephalogram, too

tiny to read. Let him be free and rich and happy. Let him
have a daughter some day, look down for the first time

at the plainness of her soft skull, her pristine scalp,
most infinite of possibilities only the wealthy can afford.

The Sense of Being Looked At

Around the corner, footsteps. A heel
clicking stone. The slosh of loose gravel

and then the no-sound itself conspicuous—
even the crickets hold their breath, hush

their rough legs while deep inside houses
women reading bedtime stories pause

to change their endings, one good wish
at a time. A car sails by with its lights off,

but Elvis on the radio still crooning after all
these years, still young—like nothing's gone

wrong. When you turn, the trees spring back,
defensive. They point to each other all at once,

a dozen limbs like the Scarecrow's saying,
He went that way. No, no, he went that way.

THE GOOD TIMES
for N.

They told me to remember the good times,
so I thought of chess in the church pew.

Over and over I relived our singular match—
six moves and a handshake. Winning the toss

he led with a pawn. I mimicked his every move.
I opened the alley, brandished the bishop like

a suicide note he stood without reading, returning
to his paper, his pipe, leaving me there

with my own mistakes. When it was my turn
I tucked in my shirt, straightened my good tie.

Read a psalm I never believed in. The choir
kicked up a few notes, one mezzo-alto short.

We drove home in pairs, ate deviled eggs—
his favorite—as if we'd always liked them most.

PLUOTS AND APRIUMS
for M.

What is missing
isn't the sweetness,

the succulence.

Lord knows
enough sucrose

will render any object

edible.
Light falls across

the wooden table,

across the wooden
bowl of fruit.

The hand.

The shadow
of the hand,

ring removed.

What is touched
must then

be tasted.

What is bred
must then

be named.

CUTLERY

for Kim

everywhere I look   there's more of it   a silver steak knife in

the sewing kit   a golden spoon bookmarking the yellow pages

ads for dry cleaning   tennis lessons   I lounge on steel tongs

I look in the mirror & a pair of forks have become my earrings

their ornate handles bounce   against my neck   when the

toilet won't flush I find the bowl   stuffed like a turkey   with salad

forks & soup spoons   the plunger won't work   I reach into

the dirty water & pull   it takes both hands & all my weight to

rip them out   I fall backward   & it's raining cutlery   bare

arms shielding my face from the tinny drizzle   I don't know

where all this   is coming from   it's like the house is

sweating metal   shiny little droplets of perspiration form   in

every shady crevice every   crack   it comes in all brands &

shapes   oneida   rowand   sterling   fancy spoons

diner spoons   baby spoons with rubber linings   knives of infinite sizes   an array of forks bent with bizarre   unnamable

purpose   some of it is cheap   but a lot is expensive   I can

tell   the junk I just toss down the cellar steps   but the stuff

worth saving I hide under my bed   I hoard them until I have full

sets   though how I'd entertain forty-eight people I have no idea

I haven't left the house in five years   so maybe it's revenge I

think   maybe the walls are just sick of me & this is all the

defiance they're capable of   I stand on my coffee table & twirl

eyeing the plaster   *well it's finally working*   I say   *you're*

driving me crazy   but the walls hold firm   at night it's

impossible to sleep   I roll over & utensils clang in the sheets

they poke at me through the pillowcase & I'm pitching them to the

floor   a blind woman in a sinking canoe   I heave & I heave until

my arms ache   & there's so much to sort   by sunrise

IMPRESSIONISM

In the painting women gather
at the bank of what looks like

a river but could be a log—
the blue-green bark foams

with tufts of sunburned moss
or waves or schools of fish

about to spawn. The women
don't care what's behind them.

Their one-stroke heads watch
their one-stroke hands hard

at work on something white—
a skirt to sew, a fish to gut,

a prayer to send swiftly down
river. At their feet two children

rustle like leaves as they take in
their lesson, whatever it is,

whatever it needs to be this time.
What matters aren't the details,

of course, but the one impression
they leave: So much to do,

all else passing them by—a river,
a tree fallen, saddled with moss—

and did it make a sound?
Do the women ever look up?

One child will cry out first, startled.
The other will say with her eyes,

Hush now, that's only the salmon;
they leap this time of year.

A Tourist's Guide Through Big Sky Country

See for yourself how easy it is on the prairie
to believe in God, in the perfection

of the human form. Lie on your back
in a field as the blue bowl fills, see clouds

scroll past like Braille. Know this message
is for you—your zenith you share with no one.

See the bare sky, not another soul for miles,
as proof you're not alone.

See the Oregon Trail Museum in Gering, Nebraska.
The ferrotypes of wagon trains, the settlers

who passed up perfectly good farmland
for the promise of something more.

Read of hunger, of famine, of years lost
in the wilderness. See the strength of their hope,

what kept them moving, the blindness of it.
Think you finally understand their logic.

Then wake on your back in a motel room
as darkness falls on the image of Baghdad.

Watch the skies turn grainy green, the crackle
of the live feed. See sparks flare up like

fool's gold as tracers guide their mortar
home. It must be morning where you are.

Drive straight through South Dakota,
Wyoming. See mountains in the distance

for the first time. See the forests, the trees.

APOCRYPHA

And then there were no jobs but
the service industry. Work had
lost some fingers in the Cotton
Gin, the Spinning Jenny. But
we had muslin, rayon, nylon;
we had cheap shirts and many
colors, the palate finally meaning
more than paint. Anyway what
good was a finger ungloved,
without the sheer stitching of
a handheld cordless Singer?
Machines meant more machines:
the car, the photocopier. Labor
was divided: on the one hand
input, on the other all this putting
out, this putting up on shelves.
Stuff needed someone to sell it
until mail order merchandise,
the mechanical mailman, hard–
wired electronic mannequins
at the register, breath a perfume,
zirconium jewels in their colorless
eyes. And so: Nothing but this.
A billion service workers, one
for each of us. The great conga line
of capitalism, call it, Ouroboros high
on over-the-counter supplements.
Every itch and ailment covered.
And still we've got each other.

VIGILANCE: WHAT YOU'LL MISS

first the mock poetic   almost random white flow of

headlights down a hill   the ribbon of red rising up like

lava   apocalyptic   epiphanic in this moonlit last

supper of the mind's eye   this faux-tribulation   this

fantasy chariot of a mushroom cloud until the words run

dry   cup tipped   blood to wine   wine to wound

& then the touchstone of sex   of course   a shoulder

a hip   unbridled   unmoored from all that should be

missed   no more mantle   no more holy shroud

sprouting limbs like leaves   o brutus   o judas   o

mother brother sister lover seen more clearly now   o

easy archetypal thing itself   living off the fumes of

your former self   living off the wagon of the body's

awful mass   drumbeats hollow in a distant feeling out

of things to say   unknown piling past the known

quickly now   a horse-length   a fencepost   iron

gate between two dark gates   & in the half-drunk boat

of your grief you'll remember hands as hemlocks   two

shores swaying as if a breeze   as if tomorrow or

tomorrow   as if a sky so black it's swallowed whole

V

WHITE NOISE

Listen. How the wind whispers our secrets.
How a light rain will speak any language.

APPLAUDING THE GODS

Why we clap at the movies
I'll never know. Flutter of

hands as the gaffer, key grip,
best boy, take their slow bows

of ascension, those faceless
angels of the film industry

nowhere around, exit music
rolling over reluctantly like

a mother making room.
A friend of mine worked

as an electrician's assistant
on *The Big Lebowski*, and

even if this were that film
he wouldn't hear. Playing

poker once he told us how
his mother cried at the credits,

every time; she said that now
he'd live forever. *Immortality*

for plugging in a boom mike,
he said, *think of that.* And I do

think of that, wonder who
here knows someone that

knows someone, who'll rush
home to a yearbook, giggle

at Cameraman Two's old
fu manchu, his hundred frames

of heaven. But we stand
and clap as if congratulating

each other on a job well done—
two hours of getting all the

punch lines, meeting the end
with just enough anticipation.

Overhead and unseen someone
changing reels feels pleased;

the ushers in the corners grab
their brooms and begin to nod.

SADDLED

Love is a horse, all sweaty suede and lean
muscle, heart bigger than its head. Love is a

dark horse, the unexpected silhouette, the anti-
man's empty field—no shadow unattached

as darkness clings to light like a dead horse.
Look: I can make a dove with both hands. Now

a dog, a horse, an elephant. I can make love.
Love is a horse sound the throat makes when

it's sore. I gurgle, I gag on a horse pill. But love
is an easy thing to swallow. Love is just horsing

around; it leaps like a wild horse from my chest.
Thank God love wears this simple shoe, and I can

nail it to a wall for luck. They say close only counts
in love. Lead love to the river; love might drink.

THE URGE TO BREAK THINGS

It comes on young and fast, first with toy trucks, then with

lead pencils snapped in half. Pinched flesh, plucked hair.
A little blood dabbed with a napkin. No one notices wounds

when they heal nightly. Smashed plastic fills the dumpster,

is hauled away, is hauled away. Remember how Jesus
walked on water? Well, we test our faith on hot coals.

If there is a God, then pain is power, but there's more to it

than that. There's music in breaking glass. We all want to be
complicated. Both the adjective and the verb. An oxymoron

incarnate: matter that matters: chaos quietly controlled.

Family Tree

The faces of the dead stand tacit at my feet as I roll
and writhe and twist the sheets. They watch my

back arch, my face turn baby-pink—*He blushes more
than me*, my Grandma giggles weightless, ephemeral

in her wedding dress, the green broach we buried her in
pinned defiantly to her nose—she's counterculture now

in the afterlife—and Uncle Bill, an alcoholic, his new
gut spilling onto the bed as he stoops to sniff my sperm

for potency, always in need of more rooms to haunt,
more flesh to poke and prod. My dead ancestors come

and go like ghosts, they walk through walls, through
time and space. They marvel at my porn collection,

how she moves her hips, her breasts, how Tide
is tough on stains. They've been around the block.

They've seen a thing or two. Now they watch us
fuck like dogs, like bunnies, like pandas at the zoo—

a scientific interest in their stealth, a good-natured curiosity.
They bring their rulers, their stopwatches, yellow pads

for taking notes. It's business as usual in heaven.
It's a lecture, a chalkboard diagram, a laser pointing

highlighter pen. To stop learning, they know, is its own little death. And they've had enough of that already.

The Space of One Nap

I killed you three times yesterday in the space of one nap.

Over and over, each death turning like the flap of a book.
A thud from each bullet, a little puff of air that could have

been a sigh or a last breath only you kept breathing, kept

looping back through a door I never remembered to lock—
more a corpse each time, old wounds just clotting, clotting.

I know what you're thinking. Yes they were your guns.

Yes it was your bedroom I ran to, your combination lock,
the string of numbers you had me memorize and recite.

But there is no sense to find in this—no symmetry, no trinity.

You see, it was only two of the three pistols—once the Glock
and then twice with the little Seecamp, it's longer muzzle-flash

burning the nose clear off your face. Your grandfather's revolver

I left untouched like a trophy or a bomb; we both know
its cracked chamber would have exploded in my hand.

But also consider the painting I hid inside while they dusted

your house, while they zipped your lips into black vinyl—
consider that quiet farmyard, that widow hanging her yellow sheets,

the slow cows and crabapple trees approaching bloom—

you know that painting had nothing to do with you. You always
hated the country, remember? You'd never set foot there.

No, this was a dream not a metaphor. This was a simple thing.

You were a flock of hands in a hall that wouldn't migrate.
My smile a spitcurl trigger I pulled and pulled and pulled.

THE BENDING OF BIRCHES

after a string arrangement after Frost

the circles   the stagelights   the outline of a body   of

an old man outlined by a body   by a spotlight   & one

might call that light a halo   but it extends further

deeper   & think: it is written of the body this buoyancy

like wood   what floats is carried away   this man in the

halo   call him god   call him peter   he lifts his bow

tucks the cello between his legs like a lover   like a child to

bed   & then his fingers on the strings   one might call

them worn or weathered   say their movements speak

though dull arcs   white stumps dropped taut from the

earth   one might say: whole   or   holy   or

confessional   one might say: I knew a boy once who

hung himself in his mother's attic   that this boy   so

quiet in school one day   became an empty desk

became a space to be filled   & maybe he still appears to

me in dreams   can you say that much?   & maybe I ask

him how it felt   if he was plucked up by god like a

sharp note   or if the world just fades out untouched   if

it blends smoothly into whatever might come next   & now

dust motes alive in track lighting   the bounce of the bow

the whine of horsehair transmuted electronically   the

cellist thinks to himself a line from the poem   thinks to

himself   I'd like to go by climbing a birch tree   the

mind a private memoir   dark space   the old man

bending the notes   bending his spine   pulling the

audience in   he thinks to himself: one could do worse

than be a swinger of birches   he thinks   worse than the

lilting of leaves   reverberation   folding hands pressed together   worse than a four foot drop   the ladder blood

red   face bloated   foot asleep   & the way he moves

my god   the way that old man moves   as if he were the

air & the notes he flung from his grip were the only solid

things   everything else swirling   fluttering

A CONSTANT LACK OF HUNGER

He like a healer
lays hands on the dash
of his new-bought Buick
straight-eight, every
door a different color,
the hood three shades of
rust—no windshield but
he thinks about the wind,
dry junkyard like a dusty
mill as he turns it over
with a grind and click.
It growls and spits.
He thinks about a dog
in back, a six pack,
and maybe it's enough.
He'll paint his motto
on the bumper:
What doesn't kill us
just takes longer.

CHEERS

They could have been us
hours ago. Two figures
huddled hip to hip in their
parkas like one big foam
finger for the sky's yearly
coughing of sparks and
spangles, these percussive
pops that stand in so often
for independence, the blank
case, the empty shell.
It took the human race
five thousand years to invent
nothing as a concept, I think,
my headlights flashing their
coupling of ooh and ahh,
their addition by subtraction,
long division into unity,
two faces to one mouth—
a numeric ideal found
faster than zero, harder
to lose. Any infant knows
the letter I, the silver look
of a mirror in white light.
They could have been us
studying the many shapes
of one hand inside another,
fleshy certainty of the body
as it tries on disappearance.
The crackle of gunpowder

through the car window,
the yellow sodium glow as
fallen angels of incandescent
ember halo their hair.
Could have been us if only
we'd dressed for the weather;
these cold desert nights,
this copper chloride blue.

In the Parking Lot of Our Dreams

It's almost spring and
    the painters are turning
        everything brown—

the bars on the balcony
    brown; the façade of
        the coin laundry where

my clothes spin clean
    another shade of brown,
        a mocha, a walnut;

brown bricks, brown
    shingles on the row of
        townhouses out back

like cookie-cut mountains,
    great glistening chocolate
        chips. Why brown? I

wonder up at a brown
    woman on a ladder as she
        guides the grooves of each

bristle across a thick brown
    drip. *Cubre el moho*, she
        says. It covers the rust.

Like any quiet man
　　with his hands in his pockets
　　　　and too much time I dig

for the profundity in this.
　　in pushing paint into
　　　　corners, the burial of one

thing beneath another,
　　whole cities of fossilized
　　　　ash—but I can't find it.

The painter reaches up
　　to draw a second coat
　　　　over the highest rung

and a bluebird tattoo
　　rises from her waistline
　　　　like the morning sun.

Three floors above our
　　heads the date palms sway
　　　　drunkenly on an offshore

breeze, drop their shriveled
　　fronds. It's then I realize
　　　　there's enough change

left from the wash for a
cup of coffee, maybe
even a Milky Way.

Timothy Green was born in Rochester, New York, in 1980. He worked in an mRNA research lab, and as a group home counselor for mentally ill adults, before moving west to serve as editor of the poetry journal *RATTLE*. His poems have appeared in many journals, including *The Connecticut Review*, *The Florida Review*, *Fugue*, *Mid-American Review*, and *Nimrod International Journal*. Green has been nominated for the Pushcart Prize, and is winner of the 2006 Phi Kappa Phi award from the University of Southern California. He lives in Los Angeles with his wife, the poet Megan O'Reilly. *American Fractal* is his first book-length collection.